DURING THE PAUSE

THE PAUSE

A COLLECTION OF TANKA POEMS

KENICHI K. YABUSAKI

AHUIMANU PRESS

The Mysterious guides me, humbles me, is me......

For Ann, Sean, Lee
And
In Memory of
Shigeo, Toshiko, Naomi, Hisakichi, Umeyo

INTRODUCTION

The title of this book comes from the French existential philosopher Albert Camus's famous essay, *The Myth of Sisyphus*. Greek mythology describes Sisyphus as a cunning king of Corinth (ancient Greece) who despised death and twice escaped from Hades. The angered Gods returned Sisyphus to the underworld to face a futile nemesis, that of pushing a massive rock up a mountain, only to have the rock roll back down just before reaching the summit and repeat the task forever. Although one's existence is a state of mind, Camus felt modern man's daily life was like Sisyphus's perpetual struggle. What most intrigued Camus was the "pause" between Sisyphus almost reaching the summit and returning to confront his eternal burden as a time for reflection. Thus, my poems reflect feelings through experiences and observations during the pauses of my life.

Tanka poetry originated in seventh-century Japan, uses a simple 5,7,5,7,7 syllable format with no rhymes or punctuations. My views of Nature, Love, Death, Science, Philosophy, and the human condition readily appealed to Tanka's thirty-one syllable structure. Some of the photos I took over the years affected the thoughts in my poems. I am deeply grateful to poet Carrie Martin for introducing me to this poetic form.

Kahalu`u, Hawaii
2021

CONTENTS

A QUINTET ON EXISTENCE.............................1

A BOY AT SUNSET.......................................3

ASPEN NAP...4

AVIAN KISS..5

AWAKENING DAWN..6

BEFORE THE DAY BEGINS.................................7

CONTROL...8

GUAVA TREE..9

GENTLE RIVER...10

MOUNTAIN PATIENCE AND WISDOM.........................11

MUSHROOM INSPIRATION.................................12

NATURE AND NURTURE...................................13

ON VAN GOGH A TORMENTED SOUL.........................14

ON VAN GOGH'S STARRY NIGHT...........................15

PALM'S PURPOSE.......................................16

RAINDROP...17

RIVER OF CHANGE......................................18

RIVER ROCKS..19

SO FOUL A SKY..20

THE KEY..21

THE RELEASE..22

THE TEACHER..23

THE TIDE'S RHYTHM....................................24

THE WATERFALL..25

WHITE TERN CHICK 26

WITNESSES...27

ON POLITICS AND RACISM............................29

ON LOVE..33

ON DEATH & LOSS 37

ON SCIENCE 41

GETTING PHILOSOPHICAL............................45

A MISCELLANY..53

A QUINTET ON EXISTENCE

I

TO ASK WHY YOU ARE
IS A VERY GOOD QUESTION
SUCH COMPLEXITY
OF ATOMIC ARRANGEMENTS
AND BOUNDLESS ABSURDITIES

II

TO ASK WHAT YOU ARE
IS A VERY GOOD QUESTION
A CONTRADICTION
WHEN HELD OF HIGHEST ESTEEM
YET THE LOWEST ANIMAL

III

TO ASK WHEN YOU ARE
IS A VERY GOOD QUESTION
IS IT ABOUT TIME
OR IS IT ABOUT CHOICES
PAUSE A MINUTE AND FIND OUT

IV

TO ASK WHERE YOU ARE
IS A VERY GOOD QUESTION
TO BE LOST IS GOOD
ITS AN OPPORTUNITY
TO FINDING YOURSELF AGAIN

V

TO ASK WHO YOU ARE
IS A VERY GOOD QUESTION
IT ENCAPSULATES
WHY WHAT WHEN AND WHERE YOU ARE
FROM YOUR FIRST BREATH TILL YOUR LAST

A BOY AT SUNSET

Top of the Makapu'u Trail, Oahu

ON REACHING THE TOP
IN THE GLOW OF THE SUNSET
THE BOY CONCLUDED
IT WAS NOT THE END OF DAY
BUT TO BEGIN WONDERING

Our youngest grandson hiked to the top of the Makapu'u Hiking Trail on the Island of Oahu, Hawaii.

ASPEN NAP

Quaking Aspens in Winter, Colorado Rocky Mountains

IN THE WINTER CHILL
BEFORE THE BLANKET IS CAST
GHOSTLY ASPENS SLEEP
AS BUSY ROOTS UNDERNEATH
PREPARE THE QUAKES OF SUMMER

The Quaking Aspen (*Populus tremuloides*) is Colorado's only wide-spread, native, deciduous tree. Its name originates from the lightweight shiny leaves that quake to even the gentlest breeze. In Winter, when other deciduous trees are mostly dormant, Quaking Aspens keep producing sugar for energy. This Aspen grove lives in the Routt National Forest of northwest Colorado near Rabbit Ears Pass.

AVIAN KISS

Lace-Necked Doves, Kahalu'u, Hawaii

PAUSE AND REFLECT ON
WHAT A SIMPLE PECK INSPIRES
MAKES AFFECTION BLISS
BRINGS AN EVERLASTING SMILE
AS THE JOYS OF LOVE ARE FREE

We live near a rainforest of the Ko'olau Mountain Range on O'ahu Island, home to many bird species. One bird that frequents our yard is the Lace-Necked Dove (*Spilopelia chinensis*). Its coos sound like *Krookruk-krukroo... kroo kroo kroo*. Watching them brings a smile.

AWAKENING DAWN

Bristol Bay Region, Alaska

INHALE A GREAT DAWN
AND HOLD IT FOR A MOMENT
EXHALE AND GO FORTH
WITH AN ADVENTUROUS HEART
AND BREATHE IN A WONDROUS DAY

Dawn on a fly-fishing trip to Alaska's remote Bristol Bay wilderness in the Togiak National Wildlife Refuge. The water is the Goodnews River which originates from the Ahklun Mountains, eventually reaching the Bering Sea. It was a gorgeous sight to start the day.

BEFORE THE DAY BEGINS

Peacock amongst Azaleas and Lichen covered rocks, Kahalu'u, Hawaii

A PEACOCK SLEPT THE NIGHT
AMONGST LICHEN COVERED ROCKS
NEATH AN AZALEA
IT EYED THE FIRST STREAKS OF DAWN
BEFORE FORAGING TILL DUSK

This young Indian Blue Peafowl (*Pavo cristatus*) visited our yard one early Spring and stayed in the neighborhood for nearly a year. We named him "Pete." Note the colorful tail feathers just beginning to appear that eventually grew to be over four feet long. As Pete matured, he roosted in nearby trees annoying the neighborhood with loud mating calls.

CONTROL

Fire Hydrant in local Neighborhood of Kahalu'u, Hawaii

CONTROL IS A CURSE
WHEN THINGS SEEM OUT OF CONTROL
NOTHING IS CERTAIN
THE ONLY CONTROL YOU HAVE
IS ACCEPTING YOU HAVE NONE

While walking the neighborhood in Hawaii, I came across a fire hydrant with multiple locks. I thought any home on fire needing this hydrant was in trouble.

GUAVA TREE

Guava Tree in the Ahupua`a of the Ko`olau Mountains

IN A RAINFOREST
OF AN AHUPUAA
YELLOW GUAVAS GROW
NURTURED BY WAIOLA STREAM
RIPENING TO DROP ITS GIFTS

An *Ahupua'a* is a Hawaiian land dividing system extending from the mountains to the ocean. This guava tree grows in the valley division of the *He'eia Ahupua'a* next to *Waiola* Stream on the Windward side of *O'ahu*.

GENTLE RIVER

Yellowstone National Park

WHEN DOWN AND WEARY
PICTURE A GENTLE RIVER
ITS HEALING FLOW WILL
TURN THE BLEAKEST OF WINTERS
INTO AN ETERNAL SPRING

In communions with Nature, the stanza in William Wordsworth's poem, *The Tables Turned*, "*...One impulse from a vernal wood May teach you more of man, of moral evil and of good, Than all the sages can...*" comes to heart.

MOUNTAIN PATIENCE
AND WISDOM

Pacific Northwest Mountain from the Air

PATIENCE AND WISDOM
PURE AND SIMPLE IN NATURE
EMBRACE A MOUNTAIN
FEEL THE PATIENCE OF SEASONS
AND WISDOM OF STANDING STILL

MUSHROOM INSPIRATION

Mushroom That Grew Overnight, Kahalu'u, Hawaii

IT GREW OVERNIGHT
LIKE MAGIC BEFORE MY EYES
THEN GONE THE NEXT DAY
A FLEETING MOMENT I THOUGHT
MAKING TIME VERY PRECIOUS

Mushrooms increase their size through cell enlargement, not by increasing the number of cells. By pumping water into their cells, a process requiring little energy, mushroom cells balloon up very rapidly. I observed the above mushroom go from a pinhead to a whole mushroom almost overnight. The notion, "Here today, gone tomorrow" means making the present meaningful.

NATURE AND NURTURE

White Tern feeding its Chick (Above) and Nurturing its Chick (Below)

YOU CAN LEARN A LOT
FROM A WHITE TERN AND ITS CHICK
TO FEED AND NURTURE
IS A PRECIOUS GIFT OF LIFE
TO BE PASSED ON FOREVER

ON VAN GOGH
A TORMENTED SOUL

Vincent Van Gogh, Self-Portrait, taken from
Beyond Van Gogh Exhibit, Honolulu, Hawaii, August 2021

HALLUCINATIONS
CAN LEAD A TORMENTED SOUL
TO CUT OFF AN EAR
WHOSE ONLY FORGIVENESS IS
CREATING MASTERPIECES

Vincent Van Gogh suffered from severe depression, with bouts of hallucinations that sometimes resulted in losing consciousness. On December 22, 1888, Van Gogh cut off his left ear from delirium in the Yellow House he rented in Arles (southern France). Shortly after, he checked himself into an asylum where he painted his celebrated *Starry Night*.

ON VAN GOGH'S STARRY NIGHT

Taken from STARRY NIGHT,
Beyond Van Gogh Exhibit, Honolulu, HI August 2021

IN THE *STARRY NIGHT*
VAN GOGH EPITOMIZES
IMPRESSIONISM
WHERE AURAS OF NEBULAE
REACH BEYOND A TELESCOPE

Vincent Van Gogh painted *Starry Night* in 1889 during his stay at the asylum of Saint-Paul-de-Mausole near Sain-Remy-de-Provence, France. One of Van Gogh's gifts was his mastery of colors. I see Van Gogh's tormented soul in the abyss of this painting.

PALM'S PURPOSE

Red Whiskered BulBul, Kahalu'u, Hawaii

AN ARECA FROND
SIGHS TO PASSERINE PERCHES
OF TWO QUAINT BULBULS
RELIEVING THE PALMS CONCERN
THAT IT HAD NOT GROWN IN VAIN

The Red-Whiskered Bulbul (*Pycnonotus jocosus fuscicaudatus*) frequents our Areca Palms foraging on insects and the tree's fruit. Bulbuls have an evocative call, a sharp *kink-a-joo* (a scolding chatter). In the mornings, Bulbuls perch conspicuously on treetops to chatter away.

RAINDROP

Tropical Leaf, after a Rain, Oahu, Hawaii

A RAINDROP CONTAINS
HYDROGEN AND OXYGEN
TWO HS ONE O
SUCH SIMPLICITY HELPS DRIVE
THE COMPLEXITIES OF LIFE

Living organisms are made of complex molecules, some having of thousands of atoms whose functions depend on water, a simple molecule made of a single oxygen atom bonded to two hydrogen atoms. Water is the universal fluid of life on Earth, yet some humans consider water less precious than gold, diamonds, money, or a *Picasso*.

RIVER OF CHANGE

Yellowstone River, Montana

A RIVER REVEALS
TO US THAT CHANGE IS CONSTANT
ONCE YOU EMBRACE THIS
EVERYTHING YOU SEE CHANGES
AND THAT WHICH HAS CHANGED CHANGES

A freestone stream originates from snowmelt and embraces riffles, runs, pockets and pools. Heraclitus, the Greek poet, once said, "*No man ever steps into the same river twice, for it's not the same river, and he's not the same man.*"

RIVER ROCKS

South Fork, Platte River, Colorado

SMOOTHED BY FATHER TIME
AND WATERS SACRED SPIRIT
THE ROCKS WERE GRATEFUL
FOR THE FRIENDSHIP OF SEASONS
STARTING WITH THE FIRST SNOWFLAKE

River boulders and rocks are sculpted by flowing water that can be torrents from snowmelt in Spring to near tickles in Winter.

SO FOUL A SKY

Brewing Storm on the Washington Coast

THE ROLLING OCEAN
MET THE BREWING CLASH AFAR
THE HORIZON KNEW
THE OMINOUS SKY CLEARS NOT
PAST THE FURY OF A STORM

I first saw *"So foul a sky clears not without a storm,"* as the epigraph to Joseph Conrad's novel, *Nostromo*, taken from Shakespeare's *King John*. Many human situations bear witness to the relevance of this quote. We weather through many emotional storms to reconcile peace afterward.

THE KEY

Geothermal Algal Pond with Bacterial/Algal Mat, Yellowstone National Park, Wyoming

A MEADOW EMBRACED
THE LIKES OF A KEYHOLE POND
UNLOCK ME IT ASKED
I FOUND THE KEY IN MYSELF
AND OPENED ALL ITS BEAUTY

Yellowstone National Park is a geothermal wonder where thermophilic bacteria and algae create colorful mats on aquatic surfaces. The acidity, alkalinity, and temperatures from 77 - >160 degrees Fahrenheit contribute to the viability of specific thermophiles.

THE RELEASE

Leopard Rainbow Trout, Goodnews River, Alaska

TWAS A GORGEOUSNESS
BORN IN THAT VERY RIVER
CRADLED AND TREMBLING
ITS HEARTBEAT ASKED FOR MERCY
I LISTENED AND SET IT FREE

I released this gorgeous wild Leopard Rainbow Trout on Alaska's Goodnews River. The fish emoted what Henry David Thoreau wrote in *Walden,*---"*I have found repeatedly, of late years, that I cannot fish without falling a little in self-respect. I have tried again and again. I have skill at it, and, like many of my fellows, a certain instinct for it, which revives from time to time, but always when I have done, I feel that it would have been better if I had not fished. It is a faint intimation, yet so are the first streaks of morning.*"

THE TEACHER

Bryce Canyon National Park, Utah

THE HOO DOOS OF BRYCE
STOOD BEFORE ME IN SPLENDOR
BEYOND MERE CALCITE
NOTHING PALED WHAT I HAD READ
AS WONDER WAS MY TEACHER

In his poem "The Tables Turned," William Wordsworth says, "*Enough of Science and of Art; Close up those barren leaves, Come forth, and bring with you a heart That watches and receives*" The content of books, at times, are irrelevant to appreciating Nature's wonders.

THE TIDE'S RHYTHM

Brown Cabbage Kelp on Granodiorite Rock,
Central Coast, British Columbia, Canada

THE TIDE INCHING UP
AWAKEN THE SLEEPING KELP
TO SWAY AT ITS HIGH
BEFORE THE MOONS SACRED PULL
LULLS THEM TO ITS INCHING LOW

Brown Cabbage Kelp belonging to the order *Laminariales* is one species of algae found in colder water that commonly grows on the intrusive igneous Granodiorite rocks along the Northwest's coastline. The rise and ebb of the tide is a sacred and peaceful relationship between Earth's and the Moon's gravitational forces.

THE WATERFALL

Fish Creek Falls, Steamboat, Colorado

IN A WATERFALL
CHORUSES OF SNOWFLAKES SING
SONGS OF GRATITUDE
TO HONOR THE SEASONS OF
WINTER SPRING SUMMER AND FALL

One hears the power in a community of snowflakes from a waterfall's roar.

WHITE TERN CHICK

White Tern Chick on a Kukui Nut Tree, Honolulu, Hawaii

ONCE UPON A TIME
ON THIS VERY NOTCH WAS LAID
AN EGG TO NURTURE
WHENCE A CHICK APPEARED AND GREW
TO BECOME ITS OWN WHITE TERN

This White Tern (*Gygis alba candida*) chick hatched from an egg on a Kukui Nut Tree (*Aleurites moluccanus*) branch. My wife and I visited the chick each day, watched its mother feed it. The chick eventually matured into an adult (photo below).

WITNESSES

Male Peafowl, Kahalu'u, Hawaii

DONT DO NAUGHTY THINGS
WHEN A PEACOCK IS AROUND
GOT AWAY I THOUGHT
WHENCE BEFORE MINE EYES UNFURLED
WHAT A HUNDRED EYES HAD SEEN

During mating season, this male peafowl displayed its striking tail feather plumage in our backyard amongst much smaller doves, a humorous scene. By Summer's end, this bird molted all of its tail feathers.

ON POLITICS AND RACISM

HUMANS ARE TO SOME
DESPICABLE ANIMALS
WHEN WE THE PEOPLE
KNOW THERE IS NO DIFFERENCE
BETWEEN POLITICS AND CRIME

IT HAS BEEN SAID THAT
WHAT A MAN BELIEVETH IN
ALAS SO IS HE
AND AS THE TRUTH STARES AT HIM
HE WILL TURN THEM INTO LIES

BASEBALL IS A GAME
OF PITCH HIT RUN CATCH AND THROW
UNTIL RACE SETS IN
THOSE OF COLOR ON THE BENCH
SEE RACISM IN FULL VIEW

A DEMOCRACY
IS A GRAND EXPERIMENT
OF LAWS UPON LAWS
AND THE WILL OF ITS PEOPLE
UNDERMINED BY POLITICS

RHETORIC IS LAME
REDUCED TO ONES FEET AND MOUTH
WHO IS IT YOU TRUST
WHEN ONES FEET AND MOUTH DO NOT
GO IN THE SAME DIRECTION

OPPRESSION FEELS LIKE
NOT BEING ABLE TO BREATH
SUFFOCATION IS
LIKE A FISH OUT OF WATER
GASPING GASPING TILL IT DIES

AFTER I ATE THEM
THE PEACH SEED AND APPLE CORE
MADE ME REALIZE
THAT THE COLOR OF THEIR SKINS
DID NOT MATTER ANYMORE

IN THE WAR OF LIFE
THERE ARE BATTLES TO BE WON
THE VICTOR IS NOT
ALWAYS THE LAST MAN STANDING
BUT THE ONE THAT FULLY LIVED

LOGIC DRIVES REASON
IN AN ILLOGICAL WORLD
A CONTRADICTION
NOT WHEN EACH DAY THE WORLD HEARS
THE HORRIFIC CRIES OF WHY

ON LOVE

THEY SAY LOVE IS BLIND
AND CANNOT SEE THE FUTURE
BUT WHEN OUR HEARTS MET
LIKE THE DAY THAT WE WERE BORN
IT WAS ONCE AND FOREVER

I WAS A SOLDIER
WHEN I CALLED HER SIGHT UNSEEN
SO GRACIOUS WAS LOVE
WHEN WE WON EACH OTHERS HEART
TO FIGHT LIFES BATTLES AS ONE

THEY SAY LOVE AND FEAR
DRIVE ALL OF MANKINDS ACTIONS
JUST TWO EMOTIONS
THAT EXTINGUISH EACH OTHER
MAKING OUR HEAVENS AND HELLS

LOVE IS IN THE AIR
EACH OF US A SACRED WIND
MEETING TOGETHER
SWIRLING WITH EACH OTHERS LOVE
WE ENDURE LIFE TOGETHER

THE ULTIMATE LOVE
IS TO DISCOVER SELF LOVE
FROM THIS SIMPLE ACT
YOU WILL LEARN TO LOVE ALL THINGS
AND FIND YOU ARE PART OF THEM

A THING IS A THING
WHAT IS NOT SAID OF THAT THING
THAT IS WHAT LOVE IS
WHOSE ESSENCE IS NOT JUST WORDS
BUT THROUGH ACTIONS OF THE HEART

1st two lines from a quote by Susan Sontag

THE DAY YOU WERE BORN
YOU WERE A GIFT TO THE WORLD
SO LETS CELEBRATE
A VERY HAPPY BIRTHDAY
AND YOUR BIRTHDAY GIFT IS YOU

NOW THAT WE ARE WED
SUCH SUCH ARE THE JOYS AHEAD
JUST A BEGINNING
OF SHARING A LIFE TOGETHER
CHERISHED BY THE VOWS WE MADE

LOVE IS LIKE A PEARL
THATS NURTURED IN AN OYSTER
FROM A SPECK OF SAND
GROWING LAYER BY LAYER
INTO A PRECIOUS JEWEL

ON DEATH & LOSS

NOW THAT YOU ARE GONE
A PART OF YOU WAS TAKEN
AND A GIFT RETURNED
IN THE PRECIOUS MEMORIES
NEVER TO BE FORGOTTEN

WHAT YOURE WEATHERING
I CAN ONLY IMAGINE
TRUST AFTER THE STORM
THERE AWAITS A GOLDEN SKY
AND THE SWEET SONG OF A LARK

DID YOU HAVE TO DIE
IN MY SIMPLE IGNORANCE
I SHOULD NOT HAVE ASKED
IT WAS NEVER ABOUT YOU
BUT TOTALLY ABOUT ME

NOW THAT YOU HAVE PASSED
AND CROSSED THE ETERNAL BAR
I WILL REMEMBER
THE LIFE YOU LED AND MUCH MORE
AND I WILL JOIN YOU IN TIME

AS I MOURN YOUR DEATH
MY CUP NOW DOST OVERFLOWS
WITH THE COUNTLESS WAYS
I NEVER THOUGHT TO TELL YOU
OF HOW MUCH YOU MEANT TO ME

IT SAID CAUSE OF DEATH
WAS FROM NATURAL CAUSES
SUCH A PEACEFUL FACE
UNTIL I ASKED THE QUESTION
IS WAR A NATURAL CAUSE

ON SCIENCE

SCIENCE DOES NOT KNOW
THE ORIGINS OF MANKIND
NOR AN AMOEBAS
LEAVES AN ABYSS OF QUESTIONS
THAT BRING MORE SPECULATIONS

CURIOSITY
THEY SAY KILLED A FRIENDLY CAT
WONDERMENT DIFFERES
IT IS NOT ATTACHED TO DEATH
BUT DWELLS IN THE IMMORTAL

HUMAN BEHAVIOR
IS NOT IN THE DNA
INSANE AS IT SEEMS
THERE ARE NO SOCIAL PROBLEMS
ONLY THE LAWS OF CULTURES

ATOMICITY
A WORLD OF DUALITIES
UNCERTAINTY RULES
BECAUSE NOTHING IS CERTAIN
AND THE RUB NOT EVEN THAT

WHATS IMPOSSIBLE
TAKES A SINGLE OCCURRENCE
BECOMES POSSIBLE
ANGERS THE RATIONAL MIND
MAKES THE INTUITIVE SMILE

DISTANCES DEFINE
NEBULAE AND ELECTRONS
SO FAR YET SO CLOSE
WHEN YOU UNDERSTAND THE FACT
AN ANGSTROMS IN A LIGHT YEAR

WHATS REALITY
IN A COMPUTERIZED WORLD
WHEN WHATS ON A SCREEN
IS WORSHIPPED MORE THAN A GOD
AND BREAKS THE HEART OF NATURE

ONE THING I DO KNOW
AND THAT IS I KNOW NOTHING
I AM SATISFIED
FEELING THE MYSTERIOUS
IN A DROP OF POND WATER

HUMAN CONCEPTION
THE INTERTWINING OF GENES
DANCE OF DNA
CREATES AN ORGANISM
OF POSSIBLE MIRACLES

GETTING PHILOSOPHICAL

THE JOURNEY OF LIFE
SHOULD BE GENTLY TREAD UPON
RAMBLING THROUGH ONES LIFE
FORGETTING THE IMPORTANCE
OF NOT TRAMPLING ON RESPECT

NO PUN INTENDED
AS THE TRUTH IS WHERE IT LIES
CLEAR AS A FULL MOON
WHEN FACTS STARE US IN THE FACE
YET DENIAL THE VICTOR

SO PROFOUND IT IS
IT DWELLS WITHIN OUR NATURE
IN ALL OF LIFES GIFTS
IT IS NOT HOW MUCH YOU KNOW
BUT IN WHAT YOU UNDERSTAND

ONE THING I HAVE FOUND
I DONT KNOW MUCH ABOUT GOD
BUT WHAT I DO KNOW
IN THE PROFOUND SCHEME OF LIFE
ITS ALL A GREAT MYSTERY

HEREIN LIES THE RUB
FOR THE LOST WANDERING SOUL
THE ANSWERS ARE NOT
IN THE ABYSS YOU MAKE IT
BUT RIGHT IN FRONT OF YOUR FACE

ISOLATION LEAVES
AN EMPTY STAGE THAT AWAITS
AN ACTOR TO BRUSH
AWAY THE RELENTLESS FEAR
WITH THE MAGIC IN BOLDNESS

THE EARTH IS A STAGE
OF CONTINENTS AND BORDERS
WHERE MANKIND CLASHES
IN THE DRAMA OF CONFLICTS
AMID THE BORDERLESS AIR

I ASKED WHAT IS JOY
AND FOUND IT NOT FAR AWAY
TWAS TO SIMPLY FEEL
THAT I AM A MYSTERY
FROM BEGINNING UNTIL END

I HAVE FOUND LATELY
TO TEACH A MAN ANYTHING
IS A FRUITLESS ACT
TO HELP FIND IT WITHIN HIM
IS A TEACHERS GREATEST JOY

TO FEEL ALL IS WELL
WHERE EVERTHING HAS ITS PLACE
IN A WORLD OF FATE
EACH DAY A NEW ADVENTURE
IN THE MANY PATHS WE CHOOSE

HUMANS ARE IN FACT
UNIQUE CULTURAL BEINGS
WITH ULTIMATE GOALS
TO KNOW THEIR LIMITATIONS
IS UNLIMITED WISDOM

A RELATIONSHIP
IS AN EVOLVING SPIRIT
A CONTINUUM
OF UPS AND DOWNS AND AROUNDS
TRYING TO COMMUNICATE

WHEN YOU ASK YOURSELF
WHY IN THE WORLD AM I HERE
YOU WILL FIND THROUGH TIME
IT CANT BE ANSWERED BY WORDS
ONLY THROUGH HEARTFELT ACTIONS

LIFES A POKER GAME
WE ARE DEALT A HAND EACH DAY
HOLD FOLD BLUFF AND CALL
PLAY YOUR HAND THE BEST YOU CAN
YOURE ALL IN TO THE LAST CHIP

WE WALK A THIN LINE
ALWAYS BETWEEN LIFE AND DEATH
SUNRISE TILL SUNSET
WHETHER ON THE BATTLEFIELDS
OR WALKING ACROSS THE STREET

TO CHERISH SELF WORTH
SHOULD BE EDUCATIONS GOAL
DISCOVERING IT
WILL BE THE HARDEST BATTLE
THAT ONE NEVER STOPS FIGHTING

A RIVER RUNS THROUGH
THE VEINS OF OUR ANCESTORS
MERGING INTO ONE
RAGING PERPETUAL FLOW
OF THE HUMAN CONDITION

A TROUT EATS A FLY
SO TO SURVIVE THE NEXT DAY
THEN WHY IS IT THAT
HUMAN EXISTENCE THRIVES ON
MURDERERS AND MURDEREES

UNIVERSALLY
HUMAN EXISTENCE FOLLOWS
A SIMPLE RHYTHM
A CADENCE OF NO ESCAPE
ONE THING LEADS TO ANOTHER

WE TAKE THINGS LIGHTLY
LIKE THE VERY AIR WE BREATHE
UNTIL TRAGEDY
STRIKES WITH FANGS OF NO MERCY
KILLS WHAT WE TOOK FOR GRANTED

CULTURES ARE THE GLUES
THAT BIND MANKIND TOGETHER
EACH WITH ITS OWN LAWS
PROVIDE THE WORLD DRAMAS OF
UNINTELLIGIBLENESS

THE DIFFERENCE BETWEEN
STUDPIDITY AND GENIUS
IS IN THEIR LIMITS
GENIUS HAS LIMITATIONS
BUT STUPIDITY HAS NONE

WHAT IS A HOTDOG
A VERY PROFOUND QUESTION
OR SENSELESS TO SOME
UNTIL ONE THINKS ABOUT IT
IS MORE THAN SAUSAGE AND BUN

THE ESSENCE OF WEALTH
IS NOT IN ONES POSSESSIONS
THE LOVE OF MONEY
IS AN EMOTION OF FEAR
TO KEEP UP WITH ONES NEIGHBORS

IMAGINATION
SHUNS THE IMPOSSIBLE WORLD
LIKE A RAGING FIRE
FUELED BY THE HEARTS DRY TINDER
BURNS WITH CREATIVITY

THERE ARE MANY FORKS
IN LIFES WONDEROUS JOURNEY
WHEN YOU COME TO ONE
ITS AN OPPORTUNITY
TO CELEBRATE THE UNKNOWN

FEAR NOT BEING LOST
BECAUSE IT IS JUST A PHASE
ITS FINDING YOUR WAY
WHERE BOLDNESS HAS THE POWER
IN MAKING YOUR DREAMS COME TRUE

A MISCELLANY

TO LIVE AND LET LIVE
IS WHAT INTUITION SAYS
TO KILL OR BE KILLED
IS WHAT THE RATIONAL SAYS
THUS WHO DO YOU LISTEN TO

CLIMATE CHANGE IS REAL
SO WHY EXACERBATE IT
IRREVERSIBLY
BY THE ACTIONS OF MANKIND
THAT DO NOT MAKE ANY SENSE

THE ELEPHANT MAN
WAS TREATED LIKE A MONSTER
PEOPLE DID NOT SEE
HE WAS A HUMAN BEING
AND CARRIED A HEART OF GOLD

WHAT IS A TRUE FRIEND
SOMEONE UNDEFINED UNTIL
YOU FACE A CRISIS
AND FROM BEGINNING TO END
THERES A HEART THATS THERE FOR YOU

EXPERIENCES
FLOW INTO A GREAT OCEAN
WHERE WE DISCOVER
THE RIVER THATS WITHIN US
THE SEA IS ALL ABOUT US

Last two lines from T. S. Eliot, "The Dry Salvages"

AS TIME TRAVELS ON
YOU BECOME PART OF THE PAST
THAT CANT BE MADE UP
ONLY THE FUTURE AWAITS
A FLEETING PRESENT MOMENT

WITHIN ALL OF US
IS THE HUMAN CONDITION
OF UNTOLD STORIES
THAT HAVE FOLLOWED THE VALLEYS
AND CLIMBED THE GREAT HEIGHTS OF LIFE

ITS BEEN SAID THAT ART
CAN NEVER BE UNDERSTOOD
BUT IS LIKE MAGIC
APPEARING BEFORE ONES EYES
BY THE VISION OF THE HEART

HOPE IS A JOURNEY
ONLY THE HEART CAN DEFINE
BUT REMEMBER THIS
THE ROADS AHEAD MAY BE LONG
AND THE MEMORIES TOO SHORT

TO SIMPLY WONDER
HAS WITHIN IT THE POWER
OF A SINGLE THOUGHT
TO TRANSFORM ONES UNIVERSE
BY THE EMOTION OF LOVE

PRECIOUS ARE THE WORLDS
BENEATH THE ROCKS ON A SHORE
THINK TWICE BEFORE YOU
DISTURB OR OVERTURN THEM
AND RIP AWAY THEIR PURPOSE

THE VOICES OF WAR
ARE NOT SILENCED BY THE DEAD
THEY RING LOUD AND CLEAR
IT IS NOT ABOUT WHOS RIGHT
BUT THE HORROR IN WHATS LEFT

A POND WITH TWO FROGS
CAN TEACH ALL MORTAL BEINGS
A SIMPLE WISDOM
IT IS NOT WISE TO DRINK UP
THE POND IN WHICH THEY MUST LIVE

WHEN YOU ARE IN AWE
ALL BEAUTY AND MYSTERY
ARE ONE AND THE SAME
LET EVERY PRECIOUS MOMENT
DWELL IN YOUR HEART FOREVER

CPSIA information can be obtained
at www.ICGtesting.com
Printed in the USA
LVHW071115200723
752687LV00056B/824